Walter Mengler

Fit in 15 Minuten

Fit in 15 Minutes

Warm-ups und Basisübungen für Violoncello
Warm-ups and Essential Exercises for Violoncello

ED 21623
ISMN 979-001-19559-1

www.schott-music.com

Mainz · London · Berlin · Madrid · New York · Paris · Prague · Tokyo · Toronto
© 2015 SCHOTT MUSIC GmbH & Co. KG, Mainz · Printed in Germany

Vorwort

Für den Sportler wie für den Musiker sind sie als Einstieg in eine Trainingsphase unverzichtbar: kurze, grundlegende „Warm-up"-Übungen, die in wenigen Minuten Körper und Instrument in Einklang bringen. Darüber hinaus bieten die Kapitel „Weiterführende Techniken" und „(Nicht all-)tägliche Übungen" breitgefächerte Anregungen, die Präzision des Spiels und die Beherrschung des Instrumentes zu pflegen und zu verbessern.

Fit in 15 Minuten richtet sich an „Wenigspieler" mit akutem Zeitmangel, die in einer konzentrierten und effektiv genutzten Viertelstunde ihre Cellotechnik bewahren und verbessern wollen, genauso wie an „Vielspieler" für den Beginn einer längeren Übe- oder Probenphase. Das Angebot reicht von sehr leichten Basisübungen – zum Teil nur auf leeren Saiten – bis hin zu kurzen Extremübungen, die zu einem individuellen Programm in unterschiedlichen Schwierigkeitsgraden kombiniert werden können.

Übeempfehlung für die tägliche Viertelstunde:

- zwei bis drei Grundübungen aus Kapitel 1
- jeweils eine Übung aus Kapitel 2 und 3
- eine Tonleiter aus Kapitel 1 als Vorbereitung auf das folgende Übungspensum oder die entsprechende Spielliteratur

Walter Mengler

Preface

Whether playing sport or playing a musical instrument, short basic warm-up exercises are indispensable at the beginning of a training session, taking a few minutes to get body and instrument working together properly. Beyond this, the chapters on more advanced techniques and (not quite) everyday exercises offer a wide range of suggestions for maintaining and improving precision in playing and mastery of the instrument.

Fit in 15 Minutes is intended for occasional players who are very short of time and want to maintain and improve their cello technique in a concentrated and effective quarter of an hour, or equally well for dedicated players to use at the beginning of a longer practice or rehearsal session. Exercises range from the very easy – some of them just on open strings – to some demanding short challenges and may be put together in various combinations to create an individual programme.

Practice recommendations for a daily quarter of an hour:

- Two or three basic exercises from chapter 1
- One exercise each from chapters 2 and 3
- A scale from chapter 1 in preparation for the next exercise or the corresponding piece

Walter Mengler
Translation Julia Rushworth

I Warm-ups und Grundlagen

1. Warm-up Bogentechnik I: Schwünge 5
2. Warm-up Bogentechnik II: Ganzer Bogen 5
3. „Justierübung", erste Orientierung auf dem Griffbrett 6
4. Warm-up: Finger 7
5. Lagenwechsel 8
6. Bogenwechsel am Frosch 8
7. Warm-up Bogentechnik III: Gleichmäßigkeit 9
8. Tonleitern über zwei Oktaven 10
9. Molltonleitern in c, d und g 13
10. Saitenübergänge, Varianten mit kurzen Strichen 14
11. Schnelle Tonleitern über eine Oktave 15
12. Grundlagen der Bogeneinteilung I: „Drei Spuren" 16
13. Grundlagen der Bogeneinteilung II: Gleiche Bogengeschwindigkeit 17
14. Lagen 1–4 (Halslagen) 18
15. Übergangslagen: „3-Finger-Lagen" 19

II Weiterführende Techniken

16. Erste Daumenlage auf D- und A-Saite 20
17. Chromatische Tonleiter 22
18. Dreiklänge mit verschiedenen Fingersätzen 23
19. Grundlagen der Bogeneinteilung III: Unterschiedliche Geschwindigkeiten . . . 24
20. Schnelles Umschalten der Bogengeschwindigkeit 25
21. Terzen 26
22. Sexten 27
23. Oktaven 28
24. Staccato auf einen Bogen 29
25. Punktierungen in drei Strichvarianten 30
26. Lagenwechsel über eine Oktave 31

III (Nicht all-)tägliche Übungen

27. Dynamik: zwei Arten lauter zu spielen 32
28. Crescendo: zwei Möglichkeiten 33
29. Klangentwicklung auf der C-Saite 33
30. Koordination rechts/links: „Finger voraus" 34
31. Bogentechnik „Metronomprinzip" 35
32. A-Saite klanglich integrieren 36
33. Bogentraining am Frosch 37
34. Flageolett-Töne 38
35. Glissando 39
36. Einfachste Übetechniken für die Koordination rechts-links 40
37. Greifhand: Flexibilisierung der Finger und des Handrückens 41
38. Variables Vibrato 42
39. Bogenkontrolle 42
40. Kraftbalance rechts/links 43

I Warm-ups and essentials

1. Warm-up bowing technique I: broad strokes 5
2. Warm-up bowing technique II: whole bow 5
3. Adjusting tuning, preliminary exercise on the fingerboard 6
4. Warm-up: fingers 7
5. Position changes 8
6. Bow changes at the heel/frog 8
7. Warm-up bowing technique III: even bowing 9
8. Scales across two octaves 10
9. Minor scales in C, D and G 13
10. String crossing, variants with short bow strokes 14
11. Rapid scales across one octave 15
12. Rudiments of bow distribution I: 'three lanes' 16
13. Rudiments of bow distribution II: constant bow speed 17
14. Positions 1–4 (neck positions) 18
15. Transitional positions: 3-finger positions 19

II More advanced techniques

16. First thumb position on D and A string 20
17. Chromatic scales 22
18. Playing arpeggios with various fingerings 23
19. Rudiments of bow distribution III: varying bow speeds 24
20. Rapid changes in bow speed 25
21. Playing thirds 26
22. Playing sixths 27
23. Playing octaves 28
24. Playing staccato notes on one bow 29
25. Playing dotted notes with three different bowing patterns 30
26. Position changes over an octave 31

III (Not quite) everyday exercises

27. Dynamics: two ways of playing louder 32
28. Crescendo: two options 33
29. Developing tone on the C string 33
30. Coordinating right and left hands: 'fingers first' 34
31. Bowing technique, metronome principle 35
32. Matching tone on the A string 36
33. Focus on bowing at the heel/frog 37
34. Playing harmonics 38
35. Playing glissando 39
36. Basic practice techniques for right-left coordination 40
37. Left hand: increasing flexibility in the fingers and back of the hand 41
38. Variable vibrato 42
39. Bow control 42
40. Balancing use of right and left 43

1. Warm-up Bogentechnik I: Schwünge

Ziel: Aktivierung der Bogenarmbewegung mit gutem, vollen Klang der leeren Saiten

Ausführung: Große Kreisbewegung, tief in die Saite „eintauchen", über die Bogenlänge hinaus

Empfohlene Dauer: weniger als 1'

1. Warm-up bowing technique I: broad strokes

Objective: activating bowing arm movement with good substantial sound on open strings

Practice: use broad circular movements, 'dipping' into the string and going beyond the full length of the bow

Recommended duration: less than 1 min.

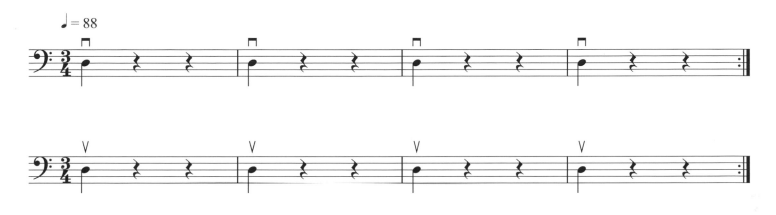

2. Warm-up Bogentechnik II: Ganzer Bogen

Ziel: Ganze Bogenlänge aktivieren, besonders die Randbereiche Frosch und Spitze

Ausführung: Nicht zu langsam, nach Belieben auch mit tremolo an Frosch und Spitze

Empfohlene Dauer: weniger als 1'

2. Warm-up bowing technique II: whole bow

Objective: using the whole length of the bow, right up to the heel and tip

Practice: Not too slow, using tremolo if desired at the heel and tip

Recommended duration: less than 1 min.

3. „Justierübungen", erste Orientierung auf dem Griffbrett

Ziel: Sicherung der Position des 1. Fingers in der 1. (bzw. 3. und 4.) Lage

Ausführung: Präziser Fingeraufsatz, wenn nötig auch einzelne Takte wiederholen. Am Ende sollte ein Durchlauf ohne nennenswerte Korrekturen stehen.

Empfohlene Dauer: weniger als 1'

Hinweis: Das Lagengefühl ist von vielen verschiedenen Faktoren abhängig, unter anderem von der Stuhlhöhe, der Stachellänge und dem Neigungswinkel des Cellos. Deshalb ist es sinnvoll, am Beginn eines Tages oder einer Übeeinheit die Relationen kurz neu zu bestimmen – zu „justieren".

3. Adjusting tuning, preliminary exercise on the fingerboard

Objective: securing the position of the first finger in 1st (then 3rd and 4th) position

Practice: Place fingers with precision, repeating individual bars if necessary. At the end it should be possible to play through without significant corrections.

Recommended duration: less than 1 min.

Tip: awareness of positions depends on various factors, among them the height of the chair, the length of the end-pin and the angle at which the cello is held. It therefore makes sense to check and 'adjust' all these things again at the beginning of a day or a practice session.

4. Warm-up: Finger

Ziel: Aktivierung und Kräftigung der Fingerbewegung, vor allem für das Hochheben der Finger

Ausführung: Im Wechsel das Hochheben und das kraftvolle Aufsetzen der Finger trainieren, von „langsam" bis „sehr schnell".

Empfohlene Dauer: 2–3'

Hinweis: Die Fingerbewegung kann in zwei Varianten ausgeführt werden: Finger liegen lassen oder „Klavier spielen" (nur der Spielfinger ist auf der Saite).

4. Warm-up: fingers

Objective: activating and strengthening finger movements, especially lifting the fingers

Practice: alternately lifting the fingers and placing them very firmly on the string, from slow to very fast.

Recommended duration: 2–3 mins.

Tip: finger movements can be made in two different ways: leaving fingers on the string or 'piano playing' (with only one finger at a time on the string).

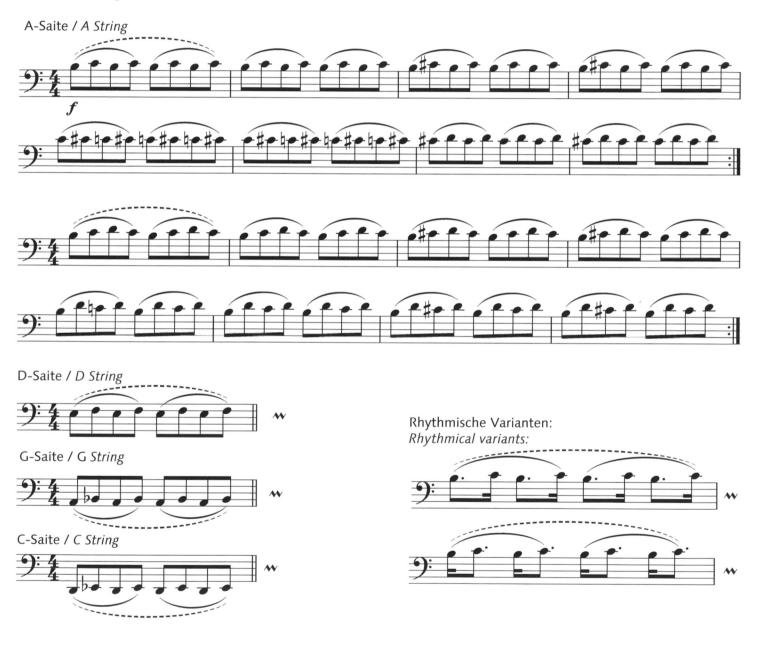

A-Saite / *A String*

D-Saite / *D String*

G-Saite / *G String*

C-Saite / *C String*

Rhythmische Varianten:
Rhythmical variants:

Eigene Varianten:
Own variants:

5. Lagenwechsel

Ziel: Initiative des Lagenwechsels vom Arm ausgehend

Ausführung: Große, schwungvolle Armbewegung, besonders wirkungsvoll mit einem langsamen Glissando

Empfohlene Dauer: 2'

Hinweis: Besondere Aufmerksamkeit auf die Klangqualität der oberen Noten richten.

5. Position changes

Objective: initiating position changes with the arm

Practice: big, sweeping arm movement, particularly effective with a slow glissando

Recommended duration: 2 mins.

Tip: pay special attention to tone quality in the upper notes.

© 2015 Schott Music GmbH & Co. KG, Mainz

Auch auf anderen Saiten üben.

Practise on other strings too.

6. Bogenwechsel am Frosch

Ziel: Lockern des Bogengriffs am Frosch (unbedingte Voraussetzung für einen flexiblen Bogenwechsel)

Ausführung: Am Frosch „trägt" der kleine Finger das Gewicht des Bogens, der Bogen wird dadurch in Balance gehalten. Beim (langsamen) Entspannen „fällt" die Spitze nach unten. Wenn im nächsten Schritt zusätzlich noch der Daumen gelöst wird, kann die Lockerung umgewandelt werden in eine flexible Handbewegung zum Bogenwechsel.

Empfohlene Dauer: 1–2'

Hinweis: Diese Übung ist eng verwandt mit Übung Nr. 33, hier die nahezu passive, entspannende Variante, dort die aktive, kräftigende.

6. Bow changes at the heel/frog

Objective: loosening the bow hold at the heel/frog (essential for flexible bow changes)

Practice: at the heel/frog the little finger 'carries' the weight of the bow, to hold the bow balanced. Relaxing (slowly) to allow the tip to drop downward. The next step is releasing the thumb too, so this loosened hold can be transformed into a flexible hand movement for bow change.

Recommended duration: 1-2 mins.

Tip: this exercise is closely related to exercise No. 33, here in an almost passive, relaxed version, while there it is active and more forceful.

Bogengriff lockern,
kleinen Finger lösen
*Relax the bow hold,
release the little finger*

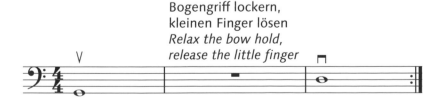

Dieselbe Bewegung ohne Pause:
Same movement without a rest:

Dieselbe Bewegung etwas kleiner auf einer Saite:
Same action with slightly smaller movement on one string:

© 2015 Schott Music GmbH & Co. KG, Mainz

7. Warm-up Bogentechnik III: Gleichmäßigkeit

Ziel: Präzise Ausführung der Tonlänge

Ausführung: Exakt gleiche Bogenlänge für gleiche Notenwerte

Empfohlene Dauer: 2'

Hinweis: Die Verwendung eines Metronoms hilft Unregelmäßigkeiten zu erkennen. Tendenziell kommt der Aufstrich zu früh.

7. Warm-up bowing technique III: even bowing

Objective: precise control of the length of notes

Practice: use exactly the same length of bow for notes of equal value

Recommended duration: 2 mins.

Tip: using a metronome will help to identify any irregularities. There may be a tendency for the up-bow to move too soon.

Auch mit gegriffenen Tönen und anderen Tempi
Play also with stopped notes and other tempos

8. Tonleiter über zwei Oktaven

Ziel: Schnell abrufbare Muster in verschiedenen Fingersatzvarianten als Grundbaustein der klassischen Cellotechnik

Ausführung: Zunächst eine Tonart pro Tag in verschiedenen Tempi üben. Später auch in Gruppen, um das schnelle Umschalten zwischen den Fingersatzmustern zu trainieren.

- Langsam (Fokus auf Intonation): mit Stimmgerät oder – noch schöner – mit einem Partner, der den Grundton aushält.
- Gemächlich bis Schnell (Fokus auf den Bewegungsablauf): Fingersatzmuster automatisieren, auch gebunden, je schneller desto mehr auf einen Bogen.

Empfohlene Dauer: 5'

Hinweis zum Fingersatz: In der vorangegangenen Cellisten-Generation war es üblich, alle Tonleitern mit dem gleichen Universal-Fingersatzmuster zu spielen – ohne leere Saiten (mit Ausnahme der C-Saite). Moderne Cellotechnik nutzt dagegen die leeren Saiten wo immer sie möglich und sinnvoll sind. Das verlangt nach zwei Voraussetzungen:

1. Die leeren Saiten müssen im Klang sorgfältig der vorangegangenen Note angepasst werden.

2. Das Vibrato darf nur sparsam angewendet werden.

8. Scales across two octaves

Objective: readily serviceable patterns with various different fingerings are a cornerstone of classical cello technique.

Practice: start with a different key each day, working at various speeds. Later on play in groups, too, so as to get used to rapid alternation between fingering patterns.

- Slow (focus on intonation): with a tuning device or – even better – with a partner who holds on the keynote.
- From leisurely to fast (focus on sequence of movements): procedural learning of fingering patterns, including slurs, playing more notes in a single bow at faster speeds.

Recommended duration: 5 mins.

Advice on fingering: in former generations of cellists it was customary to play all scales with the same universal fingering pattern, without open strings (apart from the C string). Modern cello technique uses open strings, through, wherever possible and reasonable. This requires two things:

1. Open strings have to be carefully matched in tone to the preceding note.

2. Vibrato should only be used sparingly.

C-Dur / *C-Major*

Klassischer „Universal"-Fingersatz ohne leere Saiten
Classical fingering without open strings

Des-Dur / *Dꞁ major*

D-Dur / D major

Zweimal weite und zweimal enge Fingerstellung
Twice close and twice extended finger position

Es-Dur / E♭ major

Fingersatzausnahme, endet mit dem 2. Finger
Exceptional fingering, ends with 2nd finger

E-Dur / E major

„Universal"-Fingersatz (wie Des-Dur)
"Universal" fingering (same as D♭ major)

F-Dur / F major

Fingersatzalternative am Ende der 2. Oktave 4-1-2
Alternative fingering at the end of the 2nd octave 4-1-2

Fis-Dur / F♯ major

„Universal"-Fingersatz (wie Des-Dur)
"Universal" fingering (same as D♭ major)

G-Dur bis H-Dur

Hinweis: Tonleitern, die auf der G-Saite beginnen, werden erfahrungsgemäß beim Üben etwas vernachlässigt. Zu Unrecht, denn Tonarten wie A-Dur und B-Dur sind in der klassischen Literatur häufig anzutreffen. Sogar H-Dur begegnet dem Cellisten nicht selten – als Dominante von e-Moll.

G major to B major

Tip: scales that begin on the G string tend to be somewhat neglected in practice. This is unfair, for keys such as A major and B♭ major will be encountered frequently in classical repertoire. Cellists will encounter even B major fairly often – as the dominant of E minor.

9. Molltonleitern in c, d und g

Ziel: Automatisierung von Moll-Tonleiterfingersätzen mit der übermäßigen Sekunde

Ausführung: In verschiedenen Tempi, auch mit Bindungen

Empfohlene Dauer: 5′

Hinweis: Tonleitern in „harmonisch Moll" verlangen von der Fingersatztechnik eine kleine Besonderheit: die übermäßige Sekunde. Sehr häufig kann sie als weite Fingerstellung in einer Hand gespielt werden (wie in c-Moll und g-Moll), manchmal ist ein kleiner Lagenwechsel sinnvoll (d-Moll).

9. Minor scales in C, D and G

Objective: committing minor scale fingerings with augmented second to procedural memory

Practice: at various tempi, including slurs

Recommended duration: 5 mins.

Tip: 'harmonic minor' scales require an extra detail in fingering technique: the augmented second. This can very often be played as a finger extension without shifting the hand (for instance in C minor and G minor), while sometimes a small position shift makes sense (D minor).

c-Moll / *C minor*

d-Moll / *D minor*

g-Moll / *G minor*

10. Saitenübergänge, Varianten mit kurzen Strichen

Ziel: Festigung einiger Grundmuster auf leeren Saiten

Ausführung: Tempo langsam bis sehr schnell, im langsamen Tempo auf zwei Arten üben:

1. Arm (=Ellbogen) und Bogen wechseln zusammen die Strichebene (Vorübung).

2. Der Ellbogen geht voraus, auch beim Wechsel nach unten („fallen lassen").

Empfohlene Dauer: 3′

Hinweis: Einige dieser Muster sind schwieriger als auf den ersten Blick erkennbar. Daher wird ein tägliches kurzes Training über einen längeren Zeitraum empfohlen.

10. String crossing, variants with short bow strokes

Objective: consolidating a basic pattern on open strings

Practice: slow to very fast tempo, practising in two ways at a slow tempo:

1. Arm (=elbow) and bow simultaneously change level of stroke together (preliminary exercise).

2. The elbow leads, even when moving to a lower string (allow it to drop).

Recommended duration: 3 mins.

Tip: some of these patterns are more difficult than they may appear at first sight. Short bursts of daily practice over a long period are therefore recommended.

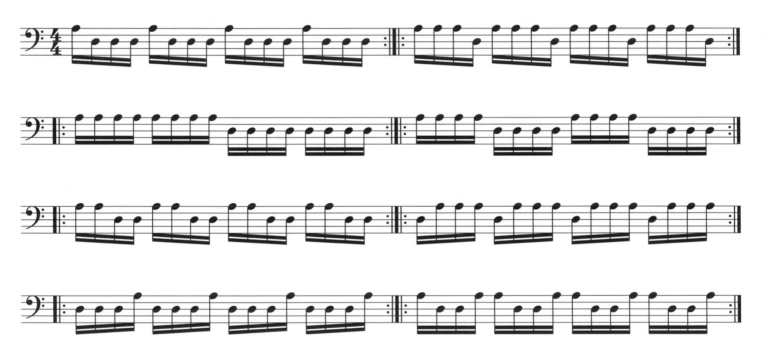

Auf anderen Saiten:
On other strings:

11. Schnelle Tonleitern über eine Oktave

Ziel: Schneller Bewegungsablauf als automatisierte Einheit

Ausführung: Schnell, mit kurzen Strichen, Variante 2 auch gebunden

Empfohlene Dauer: 2'

Hinweis: Schnelle Tonleitern – meist über eine Oktave – sind in den Cellostimmen der barocken und der klassischen Orchesterliteratur häufig anzutreffen.

11. Rapid scales across one octave

Objective: learning rapid sequences of movement as procedural units

Practice: fast, with short bows, 2nd version sometimes with slurs

Recommended duration: 2 mins.

Tip: rapid scales – generally across one octave – are often found in cello parts for orchestral repertoire of the Baroque and Classical periods.

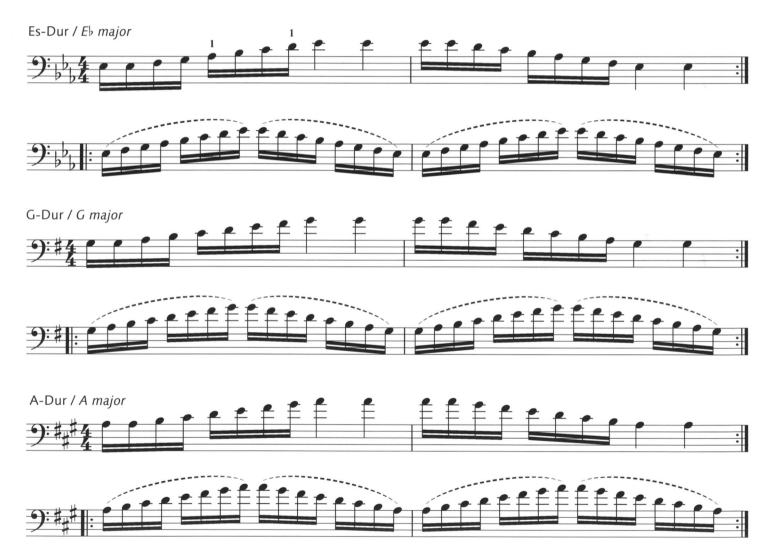

Es-Dur / Eb major

G-Dur / G major

A-Dur / A major

12. Grundlagen der Bogeneinteilung I: „Drei Spuren"

Ziel: Ein gleichmäßiger Ton im *mf* in Verbindung mit den drei Parametern der Tonerzeugung – Bogengeschwindigkeit, Bogendruck, Kontaktstelle

Ausführung: Immer mit dem ganzen Bogen. Der Bogendruck bleibt immer gleich, verändert werden Kontaktstelle und Bogengeschwindigkeit. Die Lautstärke bleibt gleich, weil in allen drei Fällen dieselbe Amplitude erreicht wird.

Empfohlene Dauer: 2′

Hinweis: Bei den gegriffenen Noten verschiebt sich die Kontaktstelle in Richtung Steg, die Bandbreite der „drei Spuren" verkleinert sich proportional.

12. Rudiments of bow distribution I: 'three lanes'

Objective: combining even tone at *mf* with the three parameters of tone production – speed, pressure and point of contact

Practice: always use the whole bow. Bow pressure remains constant, while the point of contact and bow speed changes. The volume of sound is constant, as in all three cases the same amplitude is produced.

Recommended duration: 2 mins.

Tip: with stopped notes the point of contact shifts towards the bridge and the width of the 'three lanes' is reduced proportionally.

Mittlere Spur
Middle lane

Näher zum Steg
Closer to the bridge

Näher zum Griffbrett
Closer to the fingerboard

Mit gegriffenen Noten in höheren Lagen:
With stopped notes in higher positions:

13. Grundlagen der Bogeneinteilung II: gleiche Bogengeschwindigkeit

Ziel: Genaue Vorausplanung der nächsten Bogenlänge

Ausführung: Nur die Bogenlänge verändern, die Geschwindigkeit bleibt konstant

Empfohlene Dauer: 2'

Hinweis: Hier bleiben die Bogengeschwindigkeit, die Kontaktstelle und der Bogendruck immer gleich (und damit auch die Lautstärke). Die Bogenlänge gleicht sich immer wieder aus, der Bogen kommt quasi automatisch wieder zurück in die Ausgangsposition.

13. Rudiments of bow distribution II: constant bow speed

Objective: precise calculation of the length of the next bow

Practice: only change the length of bow used, with speed remaining constant

Recommended duration: 2 mins.

Tip: here the bow speed, point of contact and bow pressure all remain constant (as does therefore the volume). The length of bow used will balance out, with the bow returning effortlessly to the point of departure.

Sonderfall: Gleiche Bogengeschwindigkeit, aber ein Teil des Aufstrichs wird in der Luft ausgeführt
Exception: use same bow speed, but move part of the up-bow through the air above the string

Auch auf anderen Saiten üben.
Practise on other strings too.

14. Lagen 1–4 (Halslagen)

Ziel: Festigung der Lagen

Ausführung: Viel Zeit nehmen für den Lagenwechsel, vorige Lage langsam lösen und zur neuen „schweben".

Empfohlene Dauer: 3'

Hinweis: Wichtige Orientierungspunkte sind die „Schlüsselnoten", d.h. Noten, bei denen man sich besonders sicher fühlt, hier zum Beispiel d und e auf der A-Saite (andere Saiten entsprechend).

14. Positions 1–4 (neck positions)

Objective: consolidating use of positions

Practice: take plenty of time over position changes, slowly leaving the previous position and 'hovering' across to the new one.

Recommended duration: 3 mins.

Tip: focus on important 'key notes', i.e. notes played with particular confidence, for example D and E on the A string (and the equivalent on other strings).

C-Dur / C major

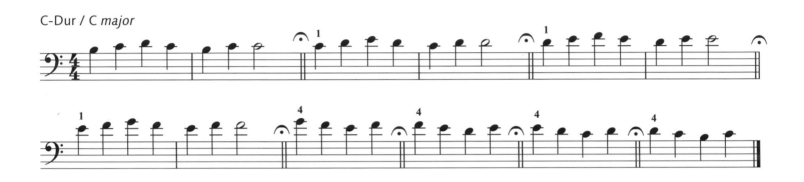

D-Dur / D major

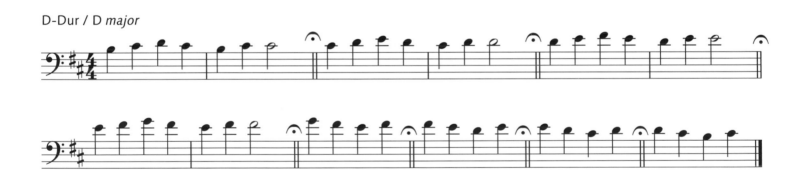

B-Dur / B♭ major

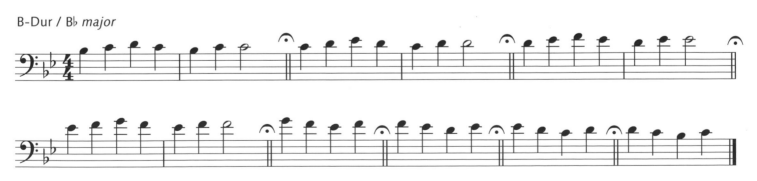

15. Übergangslagen: „3-Finger-Lagen"

Ziel: Orientierung im Bereich zwischen 4. Lage und 1. Daumenlage

Ausführung: Ganz bewusst die verschiedenen Griffarten mit Halb- und Ganztönen trainieren.

Empfohlene Dauer: 3'

Hinweis: Die Notenbeispiele zeigen nur eine kleine Auswahl der Griffarten in den „3-Finger-Lagen". Auch auf anderen Saiten und mit anderen Vorzeichen üben.

15. Transitional positions: '3-finger positions'

Objective: finding your way between 4th position and 1st thumb position

Practice: deliberate focus on various finger positions with semitones and whole tones.

Recommended duration: 3 mins.

Tip: the examples printed only show a small selection of '3-finger positions'. Practise on other strings, too, and in different keys.

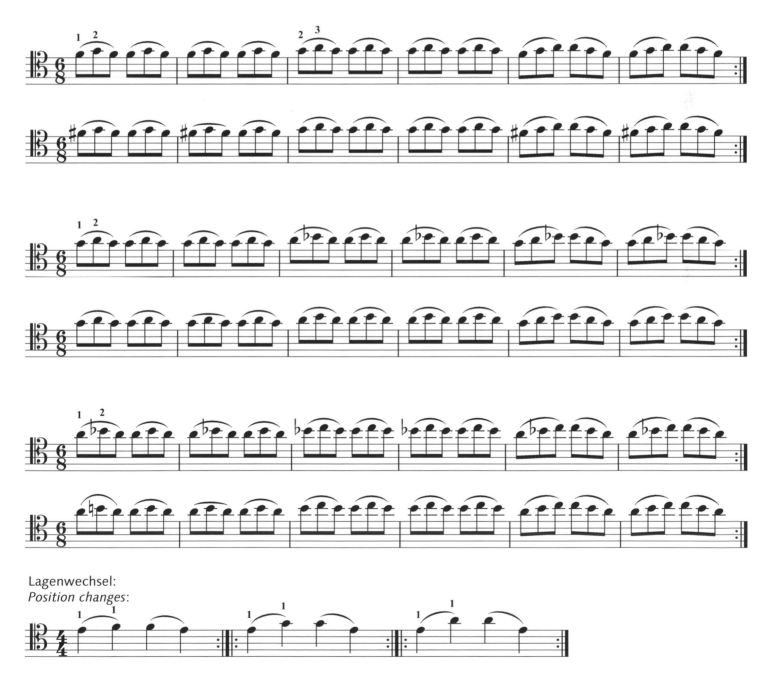

Lagenwechsel:
Position changes:

16. Erste Daumenlage auf D- und A-Saite

Ziel: Einfaches, tonschönes Melodiespiel in der Daumenlage. Vorübung zur Sicherung der Daumenposition.

Ausführung: Bogenkontaktstelle deutlich näher zum Steg

Empfohlene Dauer: 3–4'

Hinweis: Als „Extremübung" können die kurzen Melodiebeispiele auch eine Oktave höher geübt werden.

16. First thumb position on the D and A string

Objective: simple, singing melodic line in thumb position. Preliminary exercise for security in the thumb position.

Practice: with bow contact distinctly closer to the bridge

Recommended duration: 3–4 mins.

Tip: for an advanced challenge, these short melodic lines can be practised an octave higher, too.

Vorübungen:
Preliminary exercises:

nur Flageolett
Harmonics alone

Wechsel Flageolett – fest gegriffen
Alternating harmonics and stopped notes

Flageolett
Harmonics

            fest gegriffen
            stopped notes

Musette
Aus dem Notenbüchlein für Anna Magdalena
From Anna Magdalena's music book

Johann Sebastian Bach

Wiegenlied op. 98 Nr. 2
Lullaby

Franz Schubert

Sinfonie h-Moll, 1. Satz
Symphony in B minor, 1st movement

Franz Schubert

Eine Eigenkomposition?
Your own composition?

Vorübung: 1 Oktave höher
Preliminary exercise: One octave higher

Musette

17. Chromatische Tonleiter

Ziel: Ein sehr schnell „abrollendes" Fingersatzmuster

Ausführung: So schnell wie möglich.

Empfohlene Dauer: 2'

Hinweis: Der chromatische Fingersatz 1-2-3 ist leicht zu merken und von jedem Ton beginnend anwendbar. In wenigen Fällen kann ein abweichender Fingersatz einfacher sein.

17. Chromatic scales

Objective: a very rapid 'rolling' fingering pattern

Practice: as fast as possible.

Recommended duration: 2 mins.

Tip: the chromatic fingering 1-2-3 is easy to learn and can be used starting on any note. In a few instances a different fingering may be easier.

Beispiel / *Example*

18. Dreiklänge mit verschiedenen Fingersätzen

Ziel: Einsatz von zwei Fingersatzvarianten bei Dreiklängen über zwei Oktaven

Ausführung: Tempo nach Belieben, auch mit verschiedenen Bindungen und rhythmischen Varianten üben.

Empfohlene Dauer: 3 – 4'

18. Playing arpeggios with various fingerings

Objective: using two different fingerings for arpeggios across two octaves

Practice: tempo as desired, trying various slurs and rhythmic variations, too.

Recommended duration: 3 – 4 mins

1. klassischer Fingersatz: Der Fingersatz folgt immer demselben Schema, kann auch in die 3. und 4. Oktav fortgesetzt werden.

2. variabler Fingersatz: Den besten Fingersatz an der jeweiligen Stelle ausprobieren. Kleine Lagenwechsel wie in Des-Dur oder D-Dur können in schnellem Tempo vorteilhaft sein.

1. Classical fingering: this fingering always follows the same pattern and may be continued across 3 or 4 octaves.

2. Variable fingering: try out the best fingering in each instance. At a fast tempo little position changes may be helpful, such as in Db major or D major.

19. Grundlagen der Bogeneinteilung III: Unterschiedliche Geschwindigkeiten

Ziel: Präzise Bogeneinteilung bei unterschiedlichen Notenwerten im Ab- und Aufstrich

Ausführung: Zunächst mit Pause zum Wechsel der Kontaktstelle, später mit Wechsel über den „schiefen Bogen". Lange Noten näher am Steg, kurze Noten leicht, Richtung Griffbrett. Die kurze Note (im Aufstrich) bestimmt die mögliche Bogenlänge, die längere Note (im Abstrich) muss sich danach ausrichten.

Empfohlene Dauer: 2'

Hinweis: Die dritte Übung ist als Extremfall zu Übungszwecken zu verstehen, in der Literatur erscheint diese Variante eher selten.

19. Rudiments of bow distribution III: varying bow speeds

Objective: controlling bow distribution with different note values on down- and up-bow

Practice: at first stop the bow when changing the point of contact; later make change using an oblique bow stroke. Play long notes closer to the bridge, short notes with lighter bow towards the fingerboard. The short note (on the up-bow) determines the amount of bow available for the longer note on the down-bow.

Recommended duration: 2 mins.

Tip: The 3rd exercise should be seen as a special challenge for practice purposes; this version rarely appears in the cello repertoire.

Mit gegriffenen Noten, Kontaktstelle entsprechend näher zum Steg:
With stopped notes, move point of contact closer to the bridge:

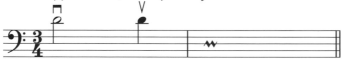 

20. Schnelles Umschalten der Bogengeschwindigkeit

Ziel: Vorausempfinden einer neuen Bogengeschwindigkeit

Ausführung: Zum Umschalten der Bogengeschwindigkeit zunächst Pausen einlegen.

Empfohlene Dauer: 2'

Hinweis: Diese Übung erscheint im Prinzip einfach, in der Praxis ist sie aber eine der wichtigsten der Bogenführung. Oft kommt die Einsicht, dass der Rhythmus eine langsamere Bogengeschwindigkeit verlangt, zu spät, nämlich erst dann, wenn der neue Bogen schon „unterwegs" ist. Um das zu vermeiden, sollte das Umschalten der Bogengeschwindigkeit schon am Ende der vorigen Note geschehen.

20. Rapid changes in bow speed

Objective: preparing for a new bow speed

Practice: for changes in bow speed, start by inserting rests

Recommended duration: 2 mins.

Tip: this exercise seems simple in principle, but in practice it is one of the most important for bow control. The realization that a rhythm requires slower bowing often comes too late – i.e. not until the bow is already moving. To prevent problems, the change in bow speed should take place at the end of the previous note.

Concerto Nr. 1 G-Dur, Anfang / *Beginning*

Allegro   Jean-Baptiste Bréval

Sonate C-Dur, 2. Satz / *Sonata C major, second movement*

Rondo grazioso   Jean-Baptiste Bréval

Der Schwan, Takt 4 und 5 / *The Swan, bar 4 and 5*

Adagio   Camille Saint-Saëns

Der Schwan, Takt 20 und 21 / *The Swan, bar 20 and 21*

21. Terzen

Ziel: Stabilisierung des Lagengefühls

Ausführung: Um das Lagengefühl zu entwickeln, sollten auch bei den Varianten die Finger liegen bleiben wie beim Doppelgriff. Die Lagenwechsel können langsam und zunächst auch mit kleinen Pausen ausgeführt werden. Strichvarianten nach Belieben.

Empfohlene Dauer: 5'

Hinweis: C-Dur benötigt zur Vollständigkeit am Anfang zwei „Einstiegstakte" mit Quinte und Quarte, weil die untere Note melodieführend ist. Die „längere" schwingende Saite (in diesem Fall die obere) benötigt etwas mehr Bogendruck, die „kürzere" etwas weniger.

21. Playing thirds

Objective: consolidating awareness of positions

Practice: in order to develop awareness of positions the fingers should be left in place even for the variant exercises, as with double stopping. Position changes can be made slowly, initially using short rests. Bowing can be varied at will.

Recommended duration: 5 mins.

Tip: C major requires two 'introductory bars' with a fifth and a fourth at the beginning, because the lower note carries the melody. The 'longer' sounding string (in this case the upper string) requires slightly more bow pressure than the 'shorter' sounding one.

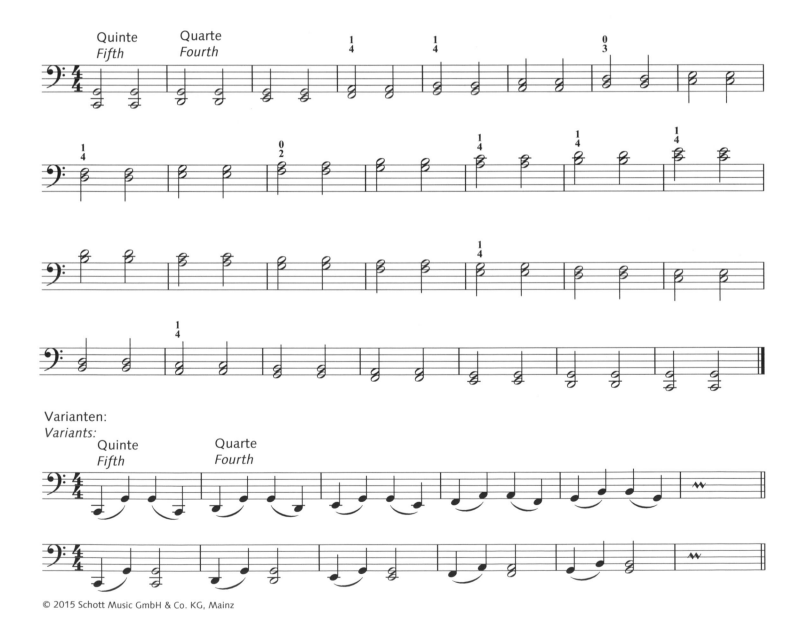

22. Sexten

Ziel und Ausführung: Siehe Nr. 22

Hinweis: Die obere Note ist melodieführend. Wie bei den Terzen muss der Bogendruck leicht unterschiedlich stark sein. Hier benötigt die untere Note etwas mehr Druck.

22. Playing sixths

Objective and practice: see No. 22

Tip: the upper note carries the melody. As with playing thirds, bow pressure has to differ somewhat: here the lower note requires a little more pressure.

Varianten:
Variants:

23. Oktaven

Ziel: Beweglichkeit des Daumens, Vorbereitung auf die Daumenlage

Ausführung in zwei Varianten:
1. als Halbtonschritt
2. als glissando

Empfohlene Dauer: 3–4'

Hinweis: Die schwingende Saitenlänge unterscheidet sich auf beiden Saiten sehr stark, deshalb ist hier die Kontrolle des unterschiedlichen Bogendrucks noch wichtiger als bei den Terzen und Sexten: mehr Gewicht für die „längere" Saite, weniger für die „kürzere".

23. Playing octaves

Objective: mobility in the thumb, preparation for thumb position

Practice in two different ways:
1. in semitone steps
2. playing glissando

Recommended duration: 3-4 minutes

Tip: the length of that portion of the string which is resonating differs significantly between the two strings, so awareness of the difference in bow pressure is even more important here than with thirds and sixths: use more weight on the 'longer' string and less on the 'shorter' one.

Vorübung für die Unterstimme, alle Töne mit dem Daumen
Preliminary exercise for the lower part, playing every note with the thumb position

Vorübung für die Oberstimme, alle Töne mit dem 3. Finger
Preliminary exercise for the upper part, playing every note with the 3rd finger

In Halbtonschritten oder als glissando
In semitone steps or playing glissando

24. Staccato auf einen Bogen

Ziel: Schnelles Lösen des Bogengriffs

Ausführung: Hier in drei Varianten, andere nach Belieben

Empfohlene Dauer: 2'

Hinweis: Schnelle Entspannung in kürzesten Pausen ist das Geheimnis eines ermüdungsfreien Bogengriffs.

24. Playing staccato notes on one bow

Objective: quick release of bow hold

Practice: three versions here, add others as desired

Recommended duration: 2 mins.

Tip: relaxing the hand swiftly in even the shortest rests is the secret of holding the bow without tiring.

Etüde Nr. 21 Anfang / *Beginning*

Justus Johann Friedrich Dotzauer

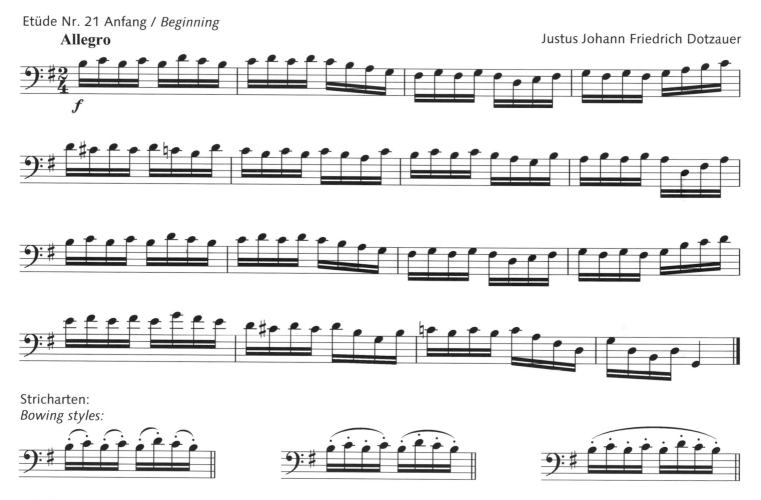

Stricharten:
Bowing styles:

25. Punktierungen in drei Strichvarianten

25. Playing dotted notes with three different bowing patterns

Ziel: Klare Artikulation der kurzen Noten und klangvolle Hauptnoten

Ausführung: In den Vorübungen wird das „Lösen des Bogens von der Saite" trainiert, damit die lange Note nachklingen kann.

Empfohlene Dauer: 2–3'

Hinweis: Die Punktierungen werden in der Regel etwas „schärfer" gespielt als notiert. Die kurze Note bildet immer eine Einheit mit der nächsten langen Note, unabhängig von der Schreibweise.

Objective: clear articulation of short notes and resonant principal notes

Practice: preliminary exercises focus on 'releasing the bow from the string' so the long note can resonate.

Recommended duration: 2–3 mins.

Tip: dotted notes are generally played slightly more 'clipped' than shown on the page. The short note always forms a unit with the next long note, no matter how it is written.

Vorübungen:
Preliminary exercise:

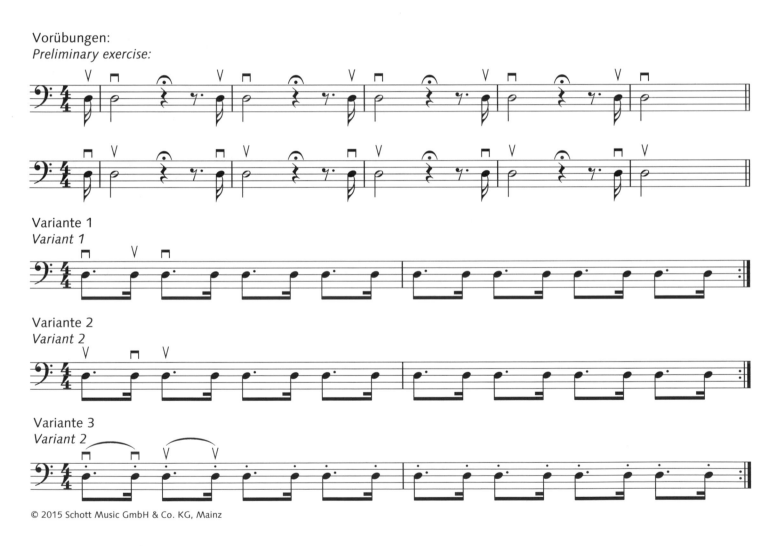

Die Länge der kurzen Note verändert den Charakter der Punktierung.
The length of the short note changes the style of dotted rhythm.

müde, traurig	angenehm, „normal"	festlich, stolz	bissig, sarkastisch
weary, sad	*pleasent, 'normal'*	*proud*	*biting, sarcastic*

26. Lagenwechsel über eine Oktave

Ziel: Armschwung der Greifhand aktivieren, Sicherheit bei großen Lagenwechseln

Ausführung: Den Daumen beim Lagenwechsel aufwärts früh genug hervorholen und auflegen. „Rutschgeschwindigkeit" nach oben verlangsamen (vgl. Übung 34).

Gelegentlich auch über 2 Oktaven üben, ohne allzu große Intonationskontrolle, nur für den großen Schwung.

Empfohlene Dauer: 1'

Hinweis: In der Daumenlage ändert sich das Schema der Fingersätze: c und cis werden beide mit dem 2. Finger gespielt.

26. Position changes over an octave

Objective: using whole arm movement with the left hand, confidence in substantial position shifts

Practice: when changing position, lift and place the thumb again very promptly (cf. exercise 34). Towards the end of the shift upwards slow down the speed of the slide.

Try playing across two octaves, too, without worrying over much about intonation, to achieve momentum.

Recommended duration: 1 min.

Tip: in thumb position the fingering pattern changes: C and C♯ are both played with the 2nd finger.

Vorübung für den Bogen: Die Kontaktstelle wandert zum Steg und wieder zurück.

Preliminary bowing exercise: point of contact moves towards the bridge and back again.

27. Dynamik: Zwei Arten lauter zu spielen

Ziel: Automatisierung von Druck und Position des Bogens

Ausführung: Um lauter zu spielen, muss die Amplitude (der Ausschlag) der schwingenden Saite vergrößert werden. Das kann auf zwei Arten erreicht werden:

Methode 1: Erhöht man den Druck des Bogens auf die Saite, bleibt der Kontakt zwischen Bogen und Saite länger bestehen und die Schwingung wird somit stärker. Gleichzeitig muss die Bogengeschwindigkeit erhöht werden, damit der Ton nicht „erdrückt" wird.

Methode 2: Schwieriger wird es bei langen Notenwerten, weil dann schnell die Bogenlänge nicht mehr ausreicht. In diesem Fall kommt Methode 2 zur Anwendung: Geht man näher zum Steg, erhöht sich die Lautstärke bei gleichbleibender Bogengeschwindigkeit.

Empfohlene Dauer: 2'

27. Dynamics: two ways of playing louder

Objective: controlling pressure and position of the bow with procedural memory

Practice: in order to play louder, the amplitude of the resonating string has to be increased. This can be achieved in two ways:

Method 1: if the pressure of the bow on the string is increased, contact between bow and string is maintained for longer and vibration thus increased. Bow speed has to be increased at the same time to avoid 'choking' the tone.

Method 2: playing louder becomes more difficult with longer note values, as the bow soon does not seem long enough. In this instance method 2 should be used: playing closer to the bridge will produce greater volume at the same bow speed.

Recommended duration: 2 mins

Gleiche Kontaktstelle, aber größere Bogengeschwindigkeit und mehr Bogendruck!
Same point of contact, but more bow speed and bow pressure!

Gleiche Bogengeschwindigkeit, aber näher zum Steg und mehr Bogendruck!
Same bow speed, but closer to the bridge with more bow pressure!

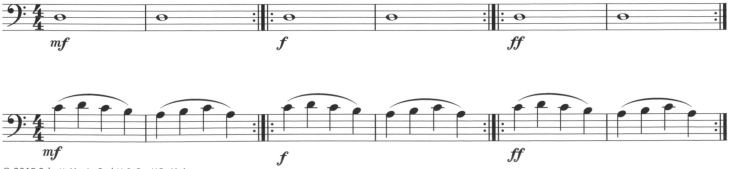

28. Crescendo: zwei Möglichkeiten

Ziel: Planung der Bogeneinteilung beim Crescendo

Ausführung: wie unter 1. und 2. beschrieben

Empfohlene Dauer: 1–2'

Hinweis: Decrescendo oder Diminuendo funktionieren entsprechend umgekehrt. Das Vorausplanen der Bogenlänge ist dabei weniger wichtig, weil die Verringerung der Bogenlänge immer möglich ist.

1. Die Kontaktstelle bleibt konstant, Bogengeschwindigkeit und -druck steigern!

2. Die Bogengeschwindigkeit bleibt konstant, Kontaktstelle zum Steg verschieben und gleichzeitig Druck erhöhen!

28. Crescendo: two options

Objective: planning bow distribution for a crescendo

Practice: as described in 1. and 2.

Recommended duration: 1–2 mins.

Tip: decrescendo or diminuendo work the other way round. Planning ahead for length of bow to be used is less important here, as it is always possible to use less bow.

1. Point of contact remains the same; increase bow speed and pressure.

2. Bow speed remains constant; shift point of contact towards the bridge while increasing pressure.

1

2

29. Klangentwicklung auf der C-Saite

Ziel: Runder, voller und großer Klang auf der C-Saite

Ausführung: Grenzbereich des Bogenstrichs am Steg herausfordern, die Lagenwechsel dürfen langsam und deutlich hörbar sein.

Empfohlene Dauer: gelegentlich 5'

29. Developing tone on the C string

Objective: full, round and substantial sound on the C string

Practice: focus in particular on the ends of the bow stroke at the bridge; position changes can be slow and clearly audible.

Recommended duration: up to 5 mins.

Walter Mengler

30. Koordination rechts/links: „Finger voraus"

Ziel: Um eine präzise Koordination rechts/links zu erreichen, muss der Greiffinger einen winzigen Moment *vor* dem Bogenstrich auf die Saite treffen. Hier wird diese Aktion isoliert und trainiert.

Ausführung: Langsames Tempo, alle Noten sehr kurz spielen, die Finger artikulieren exakt in der kurzen Pause vor der Note.

Empfohlene Dauer: 1'

Hinweis: Für die Übungen Nr. 24, 30, 36 und 40 wurde das gleiche Notenbeispiel verwendet, um die Konzentration auf die jeweiligen Techniken erleichtern.

30. Coordinating right and left hands: 'fingers first'

Objective: in order to achieve precise coordination of left and right hands, the finger must be placed on the string just *before* the bow is moved. Here this action is isolated for practice.

Practice: slow tempo, play all the notes very short, moving the fingers precisely in the short rest before the note.

Recommended duration: 1 min.

Tip: for exercises 24, 30, 36 and 40 the same musical example is used to make it easier to focus on the techniques in question.

Etüde Nr. 21

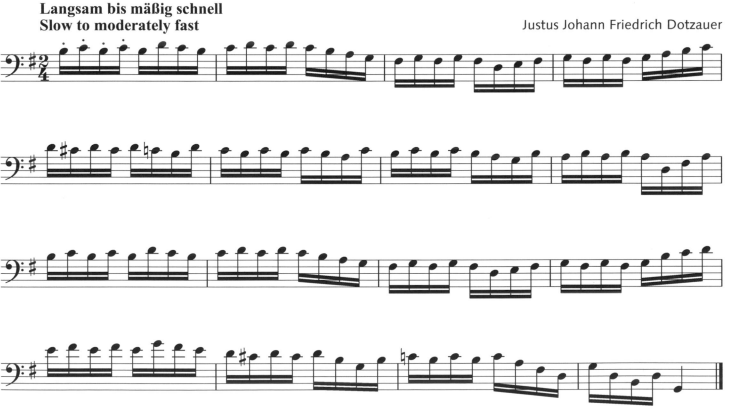

Langsam bis mäßig schnell
Slow to moderately fast

Justus Johann Friedrich Dotzauer

31. Bogentechnik „Metronomprinzip"

31. Bowing technique, 'metronome principle'

Ziel: Aktivierung der Beweglichkeit der Gelenke, Trennung der unterschiedlichen Bewegungen je nach Länge der Noten

Ausführung: Wie beim Metronom wird das Gewicht, das heißt der „Initiativpunkt" der Bogenbewegung, gedanklich auf dem Arm verschoben. Dadurch ändert sich die Geschwindigkeit der Bewegung.

Empfohlene Dauer: 2'

Hinweis: „Metronomprinzip", weil die Änderung der Geschwindigkeit wie beim mechanischen Metronom nur durch die Verschiebung des Gewichtes auf dem Metronomarm erreicht wird.

Objective: activating mobility in joints, dividing various movements according to the length of notes

Practice: think of shifting the weight, i.e. the point of initiating movement of the bow, onto the arm - as with a metronome. This involves changing the speed of the movement.

Recommended duration: 2 mins.

Tip: called the 'metronome principle' because as with a mechanical metronome, changes in speed are only achieved by moving the weight along the arm of the metronome.

Ganzer Arm
Whole arm

Unterarm
Lower arm

Handgelenk
Wrist

Fingerspitzen
Fingertips

Zwei typische Anwendungsbeispiele:
Two typical examples of use:

32. A-Saite klanglich integrieren

Ziel: Klangliche Integration der leeren A-Saite

Ausführung: Beispiel 1 trainiert den weichen, bruchlosen Übergang zur A-Saite. Das ist sehr vom Klang des Cellos, aber auch von der Klangfarbe der jeweiligen Tonfolge abhängig.

Beispiel 2: Eine einzelne Note auf der A-Saite im ersten Takt kann problematisch sein, Takt 2 mit mehreren Noten auf der A-Saite ist dagegen klanglich ausgeglichen.

Ähnlich im Beispiel 3: Zunächst die Lautstärke, dann auch das Vibrato anpassen. Die gegriffenen Noten müssen sparsam vibriert werden, die leere A-Saite mit viel Bogen „vibratoähnlich" schwingend.

Empfohlene Dauer: weniger als 1'

Hinweis: Noch vor 30 Jahren war es mehr oder weniger „verboten" leere Saiten zu verwenden; heute sind diese wieder hoch willkommen. Die leere, offene A-Saite bildet eine kleine Ausnahme, da sie gelegentlich eher hart und scharf klingt, vor allem aber sehr stark im Vergleich zur schwächeren D-Saite. Es lohnt sich, die lückenlose Anwendung zu trainieren und ein paar Grundregeln zu beachten.

32. Matching tone on the A string

Objective: integrating the sound of the open A string

Practice: exercise 1 focuses on gentle, seamless crossing to the A string. This will depend very much on the sound of the individual cello, but also on the tone quality of the sequence of notes played.

Exercise 2: playing just one note on the A string in the first bar can cause problems, while bar 2 with several notes on the A string will have a more even tone.

Likewise in exercise 3: first adjust volume, then match vibrato too. Stopped notes will require very little vibrato; make the open A string resonate by using plenty of bow.

Recommended duration: less than 1 min.

Tip: only 30 years ago it was more or less 'forbidden' to use open strings; today they are included very willingly. The open A string is something of an exception, as it can sometimes sound rather harsh in contrast with the gentler D string. It is worth practising seamless integration and paying attention to a few basic rules.

33. Bogentraining am Frosch

Ziel: Flexibilisierung und Kräftigung des Handgelenkes und der Finger am Bogengriff

Ausführung: Den Bogen ganz nah am Frosch ansetzen, die Saiten sind dabei praktisch „unter der Hand".

Übung 1: Saitenwechsel nur aus den Fingern, stumm

Übung 2: zusätzlich mit Handgelenksbewegung für Auf- und Abstrich, soweit wie möglich

Empfohlene Dauer: 2'

Hinweis: Diese Übung ist die „aktive Variante" von Übung Nr. 6. Auch auf der C-Saite spielen.

33. Focus on bowing at the heel/frog

Objective: increasing flexibility and strength in the wrist and fingers in bow hold.

Practice: place the bow right at the heel, so the strings are practically 'under your hand'.

Exercise 1: silent string crossing using fingers alone

Exercise 2: add wrist movement for up- and down-bows as far as possible

Recommended duration: 2 mins.

Tip: this exercise is the 'active version' of exercise 6. Practise on the c string, too.

Übung 1 / *Exercise 1*

Saitenübergänge nur aus den Fingern, stumm – ohne Ton
String crossing relying on fingers above, silent – no sound

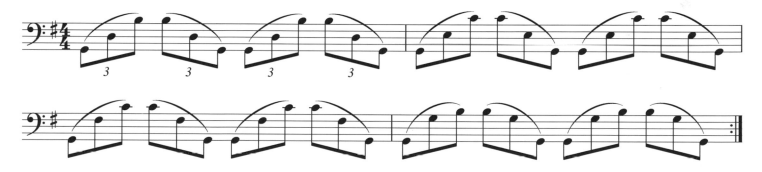

Übung 2 / *Exercise 2*

Zusätzlich mit Handgelenksbewegung, klingend – mit Ton
With additional wrist movement, with sound

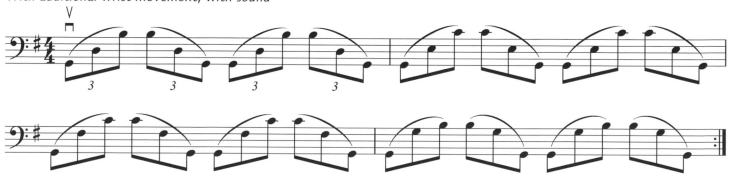

34. Flageolett-Töne

Ziel: Leichtes Aufsetzen der Finger bei gleichzeitig sehr sorgfältiger Bogenführung

Ausführung: Zuerst ohne Bindung üben. Relativ nahe am Steg streichen, fast im f-Gefühl, die Finger setzen nur leicht, aber sehr genau auf. Takt 6 und 10, letztes Viertel: 1. Finger fest aufsetzen, dazu 4. Finger Flageolett.

Empfohlene Dauer: Gelegentlich 5'

Hinweis: Dies ist ein Originalausschnitt aus Jacques Offenbachs Musette für Cello und Klavier.

34. Playing harmonics

Objective: placing fingers very gently with carefully controlled bowing

Practice: play without slurs at first. Bow fairly close to the bridge, almost as though playing forte, placing fingers gently but with precision. Bars 6 and 10, last crotchet: place 1st finger down firmly and play 4th finger harmonic.

Recommended duration: up to 5 mins.

Tip: this is an original extract from Jacques Offenbach's Musette for cello and piano.

Musette (Ausschnitt)
Musette (extract)

Jacques Offenbach

35. Glissando

Ziel: Ruhige, gleichmäßige Bewegung auf dem Griffbrett ohne Lagengefühl

Ausführung: Wie beim Lagenwechsel soll der Arm die Führung der Bewegung übernehmen, der Finger wird quasi „hinterhergezogen". Um ein gleichmäßiges Glissando zu erhalten, muss die „Rutschgeschwindigkeit" angepasst werden: je höher auf dem Griffbrett desto langsamer die Geschwindigkeit, weil die Abstände der Noten nach oben kleiner werden.

Empfohlene Dauer: 1'

Hinweis: Das Glissando wird in der Literatur vergleichsweise selten verlangt. Als Bewegungsmuster gehört diese Technik aber zu den Grundlagen bei der Beherrschung des Griffbretts – nicht nur als Vorbereitung für den Lagenwechsel.

35. Playing glissando

Objective: gentle, even movement over the fingerboard without registering different positions

Practice: as with position changes, the arm should take over leading the shift, with the finger almost 'pulled along behind'. In order to obtain a smooth, even glissando the speed of the 'slide' has to be modified: the higher up the fingerboard, the slower the speed, as the distance between notes gets smaller at a higher pitch.

Recommended duration: 1 min.

Tip: glissando is relatively seldom required in the cello repertoire. This technique is however one of the essential patterns of movement in acquiring mastery of the fingerboard – and not only as preparation for position changes.

Frei gestalten, improvisierend, lange Bögen
Improvising, using long bows

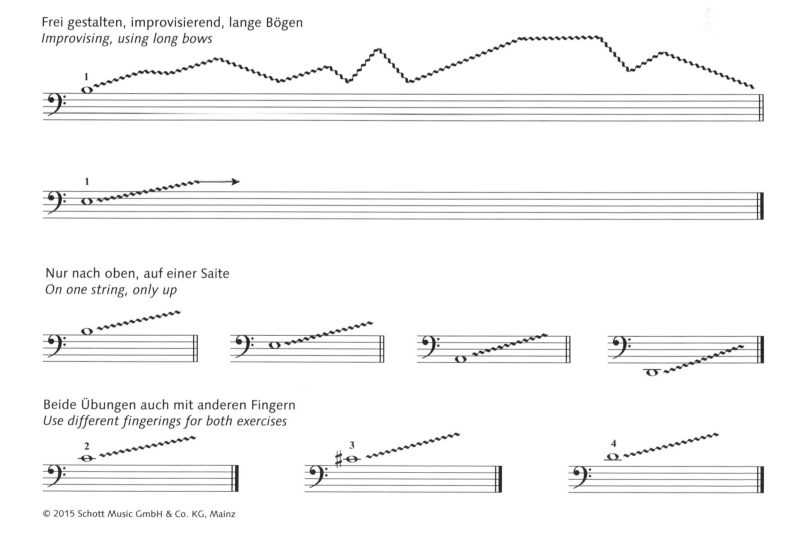

Nur nach oben, auf einer Saite
On one string, only up

Beide Übungen auch mit anderen Fingern
Use different fingerings for both exercises

36. Einfachste Übetechniken für die Koordination rechts-links

Ziel: Koordination von Bogenstrich und Fingerbewegung

Ausführung: In Übung 1 werden einzelne Noten absichtlich verlängert, um eventuelle Ungenauigkeiten „aufzubrechen" und zu kontrollieren.

Übung 2 baut einen Takt (oder auch mehr) schrittweise auf, weil die letzte Note einer Kette besonders gut gelernt wird.

Übung 3 fördert die Gruppenbildung.

Übung 4 richtet die Konzentration auf die Strichart, zu der die Finger ohne Änderung hinzukommen.

Empfohlene Dauer: 2'

36. Basic practice techniques for right-left coordination

Objective: coordination of bow stroke and finger movements

Practice: in exercise 1 individual notes are lengthened in order to identify and correct any lack of precision.

In exercise 2 a bar (or more) is built up step by step, as the last note of several receives particularly close attention.

Exercise 3 works on playing groups of notes

Exercise 4 focuses concentration on bowing style, unchanged with the addition of left-hand fingering.

Recommended duration: 2 mins.

Etüde Nr. 21   Justus Johann Friedrich Dotzauer

1., bzw. 2., 3. oder 4. Note länger und lauter: /
Play 1st, 2nd, 3rd or 4th note longer and louder:

Eine Note hinzufügen (im nächsten Takt genauso beginnen): /
Add one note (proceeding likewise in the next bar):

Schnelle Gruppen, Pausen beliebig lang: /
Rapid groups of notes, with rests as long as desired:

Strichart auf der leeren Saite, unverändert übernehmen: /
Bowing on open string, transferring without alteration:

37. Greifhand: Flexibilisierung der Finger und des Handrückens

Ziel: Erweiterung der Handspanne und Mobilisierung der Hand

Ausführung: Übung 1: alle Finger im Ganztonabstand, Finger soweit wie möglich liegen lassen, um die Dehnung zu erreichen.

Übung 2: Zusammenziehen und Streckung des Handrückens

Empfohlene Dauer: 1–2'

Hinweis: Übung 1 ist eine Extremübung, deshalb mit Vorsicht anwenden.

37. Left hand: increasing flexibility in the fingers and back of the hand

Objective: extending hand stretch and increasing mobility in the hand

Practice: Exercise 1: all fingers a whole tone apart, leaving fingers in position where possible, to achieve a stretch.

Exercise 2: contracting and stretching the back of the hand

Recommended duration: 1–2 mins.

Tip: exercise 1 is very demanding, so use with care.

Dehnung der Handspanne: Finger – soweit möglich – liegen lassen
Extending the hand stretch: Leave fingers in position where possible

Flexibilisierung des Handrückens
Increasing flexibility with the back of the hand

38. Variables Vibrato

Ziel: Veränderung von Amplitude (Ausschlag) und Frequenz (Schnelligkeit) angepasst an die Kontaktstelle und die Dynamik.

Ausführung: Großes, langsames Vibrato im f am Steg – kleines, schnelles Vibrato im p am Griffbrett

Empfohlene Dauer: 2'

Hinweis: Zu Übungszwecken sollten die beiden Varianten deutlich übertrieben ausgeführt werden.

38. Variable vibrato

Objective: adapting amplitude (size) and frequency (speed) to suit point of contact and dynamics.

Practice: broad, slow vibrato played f at the bridge – narrow, rapid vibrato played p over the fingerboard.

Recommended duration: 2 mins.

Tip: for practice purposes both forms should be played in an exaggerated manner.

Weites, langsames Vibrato – *sostenuto*
Broad, slow vibrato – sostenuto

Kleines, schnelles Vibrato – *dolce*
Narrow, rapid vibrato – dolce

Variables Vibrato entsprechend dem *crescendo*
Variable vibrato corresponding to crescendo

39. Bogenkontrolle

Ziel: Gleichmäßige, sehr langsame Bogenführung

Ausführung: Bogen 1 cm über der Saite so langsam wie möglich vom Frosch bis zur Spitze und zurück führen.

Empfohlene Dauer: 1–2'

Hinweis: Diese Übung soll schon Niccolò Paganini (1782–1840) zur Stärkung der Bogenkontrolle eingesetzt haben.

39. Bow control

Objective: very slow and even bowing

Practice: holding the bow 1cm above the string, move as slowly as possible from the heel to the tip and back.

Recommended duration: 1–2 mins.

Tip: Niccolò Paganini (1782–1840) is said to have used this exercise to improve bow control.

Bogen 1 cm über der Saite
Bow 1 cm above the string

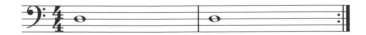

40. Kraftbalance rechts/links

Ziel: Unterschiedlicher Krafteinsatz rechts/links

Ausführung: Zunächst einige Takte mit starkem Krafteinsatz der Greifhand und gleichzeitig sehr wenig Bogendruck (*ppp*) spielen, nach einer kurzen Pause „umschalten": Greifhand ganz leicht (Halbflageolett) und *fff* im Bogen. Später taktweise umschalten und Umschaltpausen verkürzen.

Empfohlene Dauer: 2–3'

Hinweis: Mit dieser Übung wird der Automatismus des konformen Krafteinsatzes unterbrochen. Sie sollte in beide Richtungen extrem ausgeführt werden – ohne Rücksicht auf den Klang.

40. Balancing force between right and left arms

Objective: varying use of force between right and left arms

Practice: start by playing a few bars with strong finger pressure from the left hand and very little bow pressure (*ppp*), 'switching' after a short rest: very light touch with the fingers (semi-harmonic) and playing *fff* with the bow. Later on, switch over after each bar and shorten the rests in between.

Recommended duration: 2–3 mins.

Tip: this exercise interrupts the automatic matching of force on both sides. It should be exaggerated in both directions – without regard for tone.

Etüde Nr. 21

Justus Johann Friedrich Dotzauer

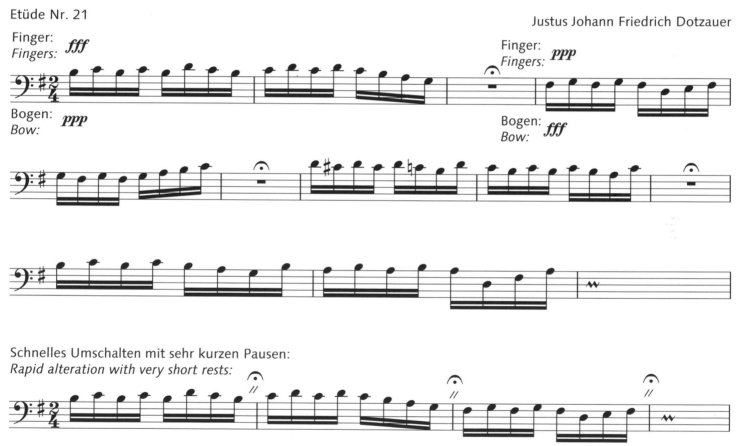

44